16

A TASTE OF MEXICO

Linda Illsley

Wayland

Titles in this series

A TASTE OF

Britain	Italy
The Caribbean	Japan
China	Mexico
France	Spain
India	West Africa

Cover *A pyramid temple built by native Mexican people long before the arrival of the Spanish.*

Frontispiece *The floating gardens near Mexico City.*

Series editor: Anna Girling
Designer: Jean Wheeler

First published in 1994 by
Wayland (Publishers) Ltd
61 Western Road, Hove
East Sussex, BN3 1JD, England

© Copyright 1994 Wayland (Publishers) Ltd

British Library Cataloguing in Publication Data
Illsley, Linda
Taste of Mexico.—(Food Around the
World Series)
I. Title   II. Series
641.5972

ISBN 0-7502-1206-3

Typeset by Dorchester Typesetting Group Ltd
Printed and bound by Lego, Italy

Contents

Mexico and its people

The land and climate

Mexico is in the southern part of the North American continent. To the north it borders the USA, and to the south it borders the Central American countries of Guatemala and Belize. To the west of Mexico is the Pacific Ocean; to the east is the Gulf of Mexico. Mexico is the fifth largest country in the American continents, after Canada, the USA, Brazil and Argentina.

The coastlines of Mexico are tropical and warm; coconut palms grow easily there.

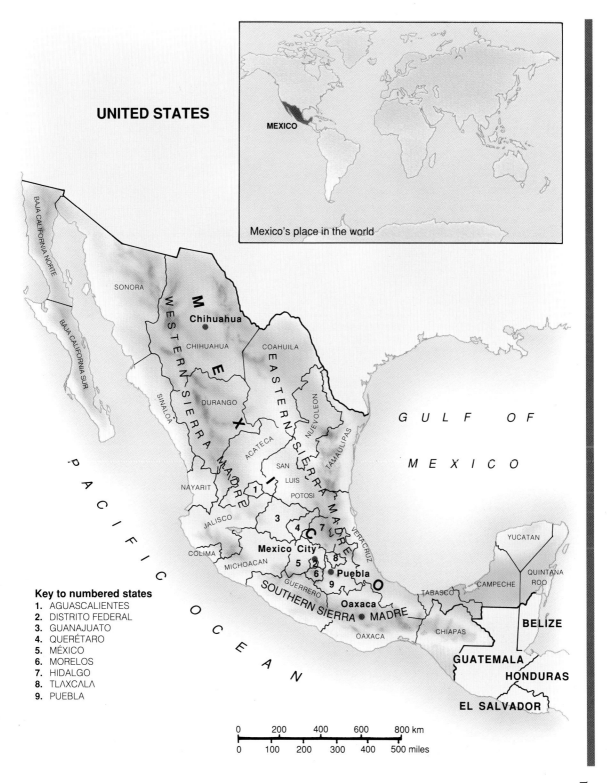

UNITED STATES

MEXICO

Mexico's place in the world

BAJA CALIFORNIA NORTE

BAJA CALIFORNIA SUR

SONORA

WESTERN SIERRA MADRE

M

E

X

I

C

O

Chihuahua

CHIHUAHUA

COAHUILA

DURANGO

SINALOA

ZACATECA

NAYARIT

JALISCO

COLIMA

MICHOACAN

NUEVO LEON

TAMAULIPAS

EASTERN SIERRA MADRE

SAN LUIS POTOSI

VERACRUZ

GULF OF MEXICO

YUCATAN

CAMPECHE

QUINTANA ROO

Mexico City

1

3

4

7

5

2

6

8

9

Puebla

Oaxaca

SOUTHERN SIERRA MADRE

GUERRERO

OAXACA

CHIAPAS

TABASCO

BELIZE

GUATEMALA

HONDURAS

EL SALVADOR

PACIFIC OCEAN

Key to numbered states
1. AGUASCALIENTES
2. DISTRITO FEDERAL
3. GUANAJUATO
4. QUERÉTARO
5. MÉXICO
6. MORELOS
7. HIDALGO
8. TLAXCALA
9. PUEBLA

| 0 | 200 | 400 | 600 | 800 km |
| 0 | 100 | 200 | 300 | 400 | 500 miles |

A taste of Mexico

Above *Some of Mexico's old volcanoes are so high they are covered in snow. This volcanic mountain is outside Mexico City.*

Mexico is a very long country, with almost every type of climate. It has hot deserts, humid rainforests, cold mountainous regions and warm coastlines. With such a range of climates, Mexico produces a wide variety of food, including its three main crops – maize, wheat and rice.

The state of Oaxaca has many mountains and is very dry. Look at the map on the previous page and see if you can find Oaxaca.

The people

Mexico has a population of well over 81 million. More than two-thirds of these people live in cities and small towns; the rest live in rural areas. Mexico City, the capital of the country, has more than 16 million people. It is the third most populated city in the world.

Most Mexicans would describe themselves as *mestizos*. A *mestizo* is someone who is a descendant of both native Mexicans (called Indians) and

Above Mexico City is in a valley.

Below Southern Mexico is covered with rainforests.

Europeans. The Indian peoples were the first to live in what is now Mexico. In 1519, the first Europeans – the Spanish conquerors – arrived. The Spanish gained control over the region, and Mexico was ruled by Spain until 1821.

Today, Spanish is the language that most Mexicans speak. However, there are about 5 million Mexicans who live in communities where more than 56 Indian languages are still spoken. These communities keep alive many ancient Indian traditions, including some very special ways of cooking.

Above *The Spanish conquerors enslaved the native Mexicans, as illustrated by this famous mosaic wall.*

Right *These children who live in the rainforests in the south follow many of the traditions of their ancestors, the native Mexicans.*

The history of Mexican food

Before the Spanish arrived

Long ago, before the Spanish arrived in Mexico, the native Indians had a very efficient system for producing food to feed the population, which was then about 30 million people.

Among the most interesting ways of producing food was the *chinampa,* which was a floating island in a shallow lake. The Indians made a *chinampa* by piling up plants and mud until there was a surface on which crops could be grown. *Chinampas* were very fertile, producing up to three harvests in one year, and the plants grown on them never needed watering! Nowadays the only *chinampas* left are in a park near Mexico City, which is shown on the title page.

Native Indians also used to grow a wide variety of fruits, vegetables and medicinal

This mural shows chinampas, *in the background, and how they were cultivated by the native Mexicans.*

9

There were many great civilizations in Mexico before the Spanish arrived. Scientists today are still trying to discover all the mysteries surrounding the ruins of those civilizations.

plants in courtyards behind their houses. Some courtyards had as many as a hundred different plants, so they were an important source of food. Today, people in small villages in the Yucatan region of south-eastern Mexico still have courtyards, but these have disappeared from the cities.

The courtyard of this Mayan family has papaya trees, watermelons and flowers.

This market has many types of fruit for sale.

When the Spanish arrived they were amazed at the assortment of foods in the marketplaces. There were great varieties of fish, seafood, meat from wild animals, maize, fruits and vegetables. The Indians carried all these foods to the markets on foot. There was no other form of land transport until the Spanish brought oxen, horses and donkeys to Mexico.

Salt and cacao beans, from which chocolate is made, were important for Indian societies because they were used as money as well as food.

A taste of Mexico

Although tractors are used for ploughing all over the country, in some areas you can still find people using a plough pulled by oxen or horses.

The exchange of foods between Mexico and Europe

The Spanish travelled to Mexico in large ships in which they carried many things that were new to that part of the world. These included foods such as wheat, lentils, rice, oranges, apples and carrots, which were soon being grown all over Mexico. The Spanish also brought farm animals such as oxen, cows, pigs, sheep, goats and chickens, and their own farming tools such as the plough and the hoe, which became part of the Mexican system of food production.

On their trips back to Europe, the Spanish took with them foods from Mexico, such as maize, potatoes, tomatoes and cacao beans, that were new to Europeans. Gradually, these new foods became an important part of the European diet.

In Yucatan the soil is very rocky. This man is planting maize with a planting stick, the way the Mayas did before the arrival of the Spanish.

Mexican dishes

There is a great variety of Mexican dishes, which is not surprising in a country with so many different climates and foods and with the influences of both Indian and Spanish cooking traditions. Each region has its own special dishes that are made nowhere else. For example, anise leaves and maize soup is a speciality in the state of Michoacan. Other dishes, such as *tacos* and *tortillas,* are made all over the country and are even becoming well known outside Mexico.

Tacos made with maize tortillas can be filled with almost any food, such as potatoes, beans or meat. The tacos being sold by this woman are rolled up and fried. The wooden bowl at the side contains green salsa to be served with the tacos.

Meal times

Above Tortillas *are used in Mexico very much like bread is in other countries.*

Mexican dishes usually take a long time to prepare because they use mostly fresh ingredients. In the past, people shopped every day in the local market; today, people in the cities shop less frequently and often go to supermarkets instead.

Most Mexicans have *tortillas,* a kind of pancake made from ground maize, with every meal. Breakfast for people in the cities may include packaged cereals such as cornflakes, fruit, eggs with *tortillas* and beans, and some sweet bread. For people in villages, breakfast may be *tortillas,* beans, meat in a hot sauce or *pozol* (a drink made with ground maize, water and salt, with chilli or honey added). Workers in the fields often have a mid-morning snack of *pozol* or *tacos,* which are filled *tortillas.*

Lunch, between 1 and 3 o'clock in the afternoon, is

These children are mixing their pozol *with water, which is a very nutritious snack.*

the main meal. People used to have a few hours off from work to go home and eat, but in the cities this is changing. Lunch might include chicken or vegetable soup, rice or pasta, a meat casserole, vegetables, beans, *tortillas* or bread, a fresh fruit drink and dessert.

The evening meal is normally light, and there is no fixed time for it. It may be just a cup of hot chocolate and sweet bread or a couple of *quesadillas,* which are *tortillas* with melted cheese in them.

Mexicans like to have snacks made from regional dishes, and the many street sellers offer delicious food. There are also special *taco* restaurants; the good ones are always full, and people travel long distances to eat there.

This street seller is offering all kinds of ready-to-eat fruit – coconut, papaya, orange and mango – which you can have with lemon, salt and powdered chilli. Delicious at any time of day.

Maize and wheat

Maize, also known as corn, has been the most important crop for Mexicans for thousands of years, and there are many legends about how people first came to eat this grain. According to one Aztec legend, Quetzalcoatl – an Aztec god – turned himself into a red ant and stole the sacred maize seeds from other gods. He brought the maize as a gift to the humans so they could feed themselves. Even today, in Indian villages, the first ears of maize that are harvested are offered to the god Quetzalcoatl to thank him for his gift of maize.

Can you see the ear of corn growing on this maize plant?

Maize is a cereal that grows in almost all types of climate. Every part of the maize plant is used – as food, fuel or medicine. Even the worms that eat the maize and the fungus that grows on it are considered very special foods.

There are about 2,000 Mexican recipes for using maize. It is easy to cook with maize because it goes well with many other foods, such as beans or chillies. Maize is used dried or fresh, made into a main course, a soup, a pudding or a drink. Most importantly, it is ground into flour and used to make *tortillas.*

In the past, *tortillas* were made in every house. If you walked down the

Above *Maize grains vary in colour. When dry like this they can be stored for a long time and used as seed or as food.*

Traditionally maize was ground by hand in metates *(see page 34) and the* tortillas *were then patted out by hand and cooked over a wood fire.*

street very early in the morning you would hear the gentle 'pat-pat' sound of *tortillas* being made by hand. Today, *tortillas* are usually made by a machine, and it is quite common to see people queuing to buy fresh *tortillas* just before lunch. Handmade *tortillas* are now a treat for special occasions.

Once the maize is harvested the stalks are dried and used as fodder for animals.

Wheat, which is grown in the north, is used to make all kinds of pastries, cakes and sweet or savoury breads. Bakers often work all night to make the next day's bread, so if you get to the bakery or the market early in the morning, the bread is still hot from the oven.

A speciality in the north is *tortillas* made with wheat flour. Wheat *tortillas,* which are whiter and much bigger than maize *tortillas,* are used in the same way as maize *tortillas* but in different dishes. The *burrito,* a wheat *tortilla* often filled with rice, beans, meat and chilli sauce, is very popular in the USA.

Wheat tortillas

Equipment

mixing bowl
tea-cloth
rolling pin
cast-iron griddle
   or heavy-based
   frying pan
spatula

Ingredients
Makes 12

230 g all-purpose
   flour, sifted
60 g lard
1 teaspoon salt
125 ml warm
   water

1 Put the flour in
the bowl and rub
the lard into the
flour with your
fingers.

A taste of Mexico

2   Dissolve the salt in the water and add it to the flour mixture.

3   Knead the dough well for about 5 minutes. Cover with a tea-cloth and set it aside for about 2 hours.

Always ask an adult to help you when working with a cooker.

4   Heat the griddle or frying pan over a low heat.

5   Knead the dough again for 2 minutes, then take a small piece of dough and make a ball about 4 cm in diameter. Press the ball out on a floured surface and roll it out into a circle about 18 cm in diameter. It should be paper thin.

6   Place the *tortilla* carefully on the griddle (remember it is hot) and leave it for about 20 seconds. Turn the *tortilla* over with the spatula and cook the other side for about 15 seconds. You can eat *tortillas* straight away or save them to be used later.

Quesadillas

Equipment

grater
cast-iron griddle
   or frying pan
spatula
3 plates

Ingredients
Serves 2

4 wheat *tortillas*
100 g mature
   cheddar
   cheese

1   Place the grater over a plate and grate the cheese. Divide the cheese into four equal portions.

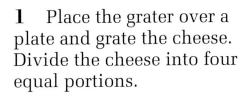

A taste of Mexico

2 Heat the griddle or frying pan over a medium heat. Place a *tortilla* on the griddle for about 5 seconds, to make it soft. Use the spatula to put the *tortilla* onto a plate.

Always ask an adult to help you when working with a cooker.

4 Place it back on the griddle and cook it until the cheese melts. Turn it over, with the spatula, a few times so that it does not burn, then put it on a plate.

3 Put one portion of the grated cheese inside the *tortilla* and fold it over.

5 Use the remaining *tortillas* and cheese to make three more *quesadillas*. Eat them after they have cooled down a little. Try them with a little *salsa* (see recipe on page 41)!

Meat, fish and other delicacies

Mexicans eat more beef and pork than any other type of meat. Far more beef is eaten in the north of the country, where there is plenty of grassland for cattle, than in the central or southern areas where grazing land is scarce. People in these areas eat pork, chicken and turkey. Goat and mutton are popular for Sunday lunch, and they are often cooked in a spicy sauce.

Above *Meat is also sold in markets. Pork crackling and spicy sausages called* chorizo *are a special treat.*

Left *Beef and goat meat are very popular in Mexico.*

23

A taste of Mexico

This family is selling live iguanas, which are used to make delicious soups.

Deer, snake and iguana meat are eaten in places near the coasts. Some people believe that snake and iguana meat can be used to treat all kinds of illnesses.

In areas near the sea, people eat lots of fish and seafood. Fresh red snapper, one of the most popular fish, is delicious when fried with garlic. Seafood such as conch, clams and sea urchins are considered delicacies.

In the last few years, people have begun to farm carp, freshwater bass and oysters, and they are becoming popular all over the country.

For hundreds of years, some insects, such as grasshoppers, have been part of the diet in the south-western state of Oaxaca (pronounced wha-hacka). Visitors to the market in Oaxaca City may be surprised to find piles of grilled grasshoppers, but if they try them, they discover that grasshoppers are very tasty – and they are good for you.

The seafood stall in the market is selling octopus and various types of prawns.

Dairy products

The native people of Mexico learned how to make cheese from the Spanish. Cheese goes very well with maize and chilli, so it was quickly adapted into Mexican cooking.

Today, there are many types of Mexican cheeses for sale in supermarkets or in local markets, where they can sometimes be bought from the people who made them.

Chihuahua cheese is made by German Mennonite communities outside Chihuahua City in northern Mexico. This cheese is slightly acid and has a very creamy texture. It is used to stuff chillies or melt over food. *Adobera,* a slightly salty cheese, melts easily, which makes it ideal for *quesadillas.* *Anejo* cheese is aged and has a wonderful salty flavour and crumbly texture. It is perfect on many Mexican dishes such as *tacos* and refried beans.

Cheese is very popular and is used for many typical dishes.

Chillies and other spices

Chillies were first grown in Mexico, where there are around a hundred different varieties. Chillies vary in size, shape, colour and flavour. Each area has a type of chilli that is grown locally and used in the cooking of that area. In the Yucatan region, people like to use the very fiery *habanero* chilli in their sauces; whereas in the state of Sonora, they like a mild green chilli.

Chillies can be used fresh or dried. Once dried, the flavour, colour and name of the chilli changes, as well as its use. For example, the fresh green *poblano* chilli is used to make stuffed chillies. Once it is dried, it is called *ancho* chilli, has a deep reddish-brown colour and is used to make sauces such as the famous *mole* from Puebla (see page 37.)

In most restaurants and at most family meals, at least one kind of *salsa,* or sauce, made with chillies is on the table. In Mexico, sauces are used to give food a

Far left *Chillies are used fresh, dried or pickled. In the picture on page 26 you can see just a few of the different sizes, shapes and colours of chillies.*

This one stall in the market is selling about thirty different kinds of chillies.

A taste of Mexico

You have to take great care when cooking with chillies because they can irritate your skin, eyes, mouth or any part of the body they touch.

Achiote *seeds are bright red. In Mexico they are used as a seasoning for food, while in other countries they are used as a colouring.*

more interesting flavour, just as salt and pepper are used in other countries. There are hundreds of sauces, and much of the time they are simply made with whatever ingredients are available.

Although chillies are very popular, not all Mexican cooking is hot and spicy. Many dishes, such as courgettes in a cream and cinnamon sauce, have very delicate flavours and are not hot at all. Mexican cooking uses lots of different herbs and spices. Fresh coriander is a very popular herb for making sauces. There are about 13 different types of oregano used in the various regions, each claiming that their type is the most flavourful. *Epazote* is a strong-tasting herb, known in English as Mexican tea. It is used mostly in central and southern Mexico to flavour black beans and soups. It has a slightly musty flavour that takes some getting used to, but once people have had *epazote* a few times, they develop a taste for it.

Achiote has a very special flavour. This small red seed from the *annato* tree is ground to a paste and mixed with other spices as a seasoning for meat and fish. A dish called *cochinita pibil* is made with suckling pig covered in *achiote* paste and the juice of bitter oranges, wrapped in banana leaves and cooked in an underground oven for many hours. It is worth travelling to the Yucatan just to taste *cochinita pibil.*

Beans

Beans, like maize, are part of most Mexican meals. They go very well with meat, rice and chilli. There are many ways of cooking beans, and almost every region has its own special bean dish. Most people agree that it is best to cook beans in a clay pot, over a slow fire for a long time, sometimes up to 3 hours. Beans cooked this way are a favourite treat, especially with homemade *tortillas* and *salsa*.

There are many types of beans in Mexico. They come in all sizes and colours, such as the small black bean, the large white fava bean, and the 'may flower' bean, which is a slightly purple bean with brown speckles.

May flower beans are used to make Mexican refried beans. People often wonder why they have been fried twice. In fact, 'refried' is a misleading translation of the Spanish word *refrito*, which means 'thoroughly fried'.

Some beans are sold dry in the market. There are many types to choose from depending on what dish they are going to be used for.

Other favourite foods

Vegetables and fruit

Tomatoes and onions are used in many Mexican dishes. They are often blended to make tomato sauce for eggs, pasta, rice, vegetables or meat. Courgettes are a popular vegetable, and even the flowers are eaten fried or as a filling for *tacos.* In central Mexico, pumpkins, sweet potatoes and a special kind of banana are cooked with brown sugar and served with milk for breakfast.

Courgette flowers are cooked with onions and cheese and used as a filling for tacos, *which is not only delicious to eat but also pretty to look at.*

Above Cooked cactus joints.

Left A nopal cactus plant with prickly pears.

Below Custard marrows can now be bought in some supermarkets in Britain and the USA.

Other very popular vegetables are *nopal* cactus joints, which are delicious when served as a salad mixed with tomatoes, coriander and chillies, and custard marrow, which is good when baked in layers with egg and cheese.

If you ever visit a market in Mexico, you will be pleasantly surprised at the wonderful selection of fruits. There are many varieties of mangoes, papayas and bananas. There is even a banana with a seed in it and another that is fried and served with savoury food. Many fruits do not travel well, so they are not well known outside Mexico.

You can even buy freshly made orange juice from street sellers in some Mexican cities.

Drinks

Because of the warm climate, cold drinks are an important part of the Mexican diet. In most cities, special stores sell a wide variety of fresh fruit juices. Papaya and orange is a favourite. Sometimes fruits are blended with milk and cereals to make a more nutritious drink, which in other countries is called a smoothie (see recipe on page 39).

Some cold drinks are made with water, sugar, ice and flavourings such as ground rice, hibiscus or fruit. The supermarkets sell concentrates that are mixed with water, but they do not taste as good as homemade drinks. As in almost every country around the world, sugary soft drinks are very popular, especially served cold.

After a meal people often have coffee. It may be instant coffee from the supermarket or freshly ground coffee from a local shop. In some places, coffee is made in an earthenware pot and cinnamon is added.

Chocolate

Hot chocolate is said to have been the favourite drink of the Aztec king Montezuma. The word chocolate comes from the Aztec words *xoco,* meaning 'bitter', and *atl,* meaning 'water'. The chocolate drink, or 'bitter water', that the Aztecs drank was made with water, not milk, and it was not as sweet as the chocolate you eat in sweets, which have lots of sugar added. The Aztecs made chocolate by roasting the cacao beans and grinding them into a powder. They mixed the chocolate with perfumed flowers, honey and vanilla and made it into different colours – red, white, orange and even black.

The Spanish did not like chocolate at first. Eventually they got used to the flavour, and hot chocolate became a favourite drink.

Cacao beans grow in pods like the ones in this picture. Did you ever imagine that chocolate came from a plant like this?

Cooking utensils

This woman is grinding maize in a metate, *she lives too far away from a city where she could easily buy it already ground.*

The most important cooking utensil for a long time was the *metate.* This is a sloping rectangular piece of volcanic rock, about 30 by 40 cm, with three legs. The *metate* is used to grind grains, especially maize for making *tortillas,* and chillies. The grains or chillies are placed on the *metate* and ground by pushing another long stone, also made from volcanic rock, against the *metate.*

In some small villages, people still grind food with the *metate,* but it is being gradually replaced by electric food mills.

The *molcajete* (pronounced moll-cah-hettay) is the Mexican version of a mortar and pestle. It is also made of volcanic rock and has the shape of a bowl with three short legs. The *molcajete* is used to grind spices and make sauces. Many people say that the best sauces are always the ones made in a *molcajete.*

Although many homes still have a *molcajete,* it is probably only used on

Many people in the towns and cities have modern kitchens and now make their salsas *using an electric blender instead of the traditional* molcajete.

special occasions, since most people in the cities have electric blenders.

Today, many homes in the cities have cookers with ovens, and even microwave ovens. Yet in some places, cooking is still done on wood-fired stoves made out of clay. In the Maya areas in the south, people still cook in underground ovens called *pibs.* Cooking this way is very slow; sometimes it takes up to 12 hours for the food to be ready. But the results, such as *cochinita pibil,* are worth waiting for.

In some places people still cook with wood. Many people claim that food cooked in this way tastes better than the food cooked over gas cookers.

Festive foods

For some fiestas *children and adults dress up in traditional costumes similar to those worn by the Indians hundreds of years ago.*

Food and music are always central to Mexican celebrations, or *fiestas,* and there are lots of celebrations in Mexico. Most Mexicans are Roman Catholics, so they celebrate all the major Church holy days. For each person there are at least two days to celebrate during the year – a birthday and, if he or she has been named after a saint, a saint's day.

Baptisms and weddings are big events. In the cities, a large hall and caterers are hired for the occasion. In the villages, all the women get together two or three days before the party to start preparing the food.

Perhaps the most popular festive dish is *mole,* which is made with about 28 different ingredients, including several kinds of dried chillies and a small amount of chocolate. The other ingredients may include almonds, *tortillas,* sesame seeds, chicken stock, onions, garlic, cloves, cinnamon and bread. However, one of the traditions associated with *mole* is that each cook has his or her own special recipe. *Mole* is usually served with chicken or turkey, rice and beans.

Each region has certain dishes that are eaten on special occasions. In Mexico City people sometimes have stuffed chillies with a walnut and cream sauce, and in some states, such as Michoacan and Guerrero, they have a soup made with a type of dried maize, called hominy, chillies and three types of meat. *Guacamole* (an avocado dip), refried beans and fried *tortilla* pieces are typical snacks during *fiestas.*

There are many other reasons for *fiestas.* Each region has different events to celebrate, depending on its local

This picture shows what chillies with walnut and cream sauce look like. The red pomegranate seeds on top, are used for contrast with the green chillies and the white sauce. Red, green and white are the colours of the Mexican flag.

A taste of Mexico

These sugar and chocolate skulls are made for the Day of the Dead. You can have a friend's name written on the strip on the forehead and give it as a present.

history. There are also national celebrations, such as Christmas, Easter, or the Day of the Dead (1 to 2 November) shared by everyone throughout Mexico.

The Day of the Dead has its roots in a mixture of Spanish and Indian cultures. It is not a sad day; it is a happy occasion when, according to belief, the souls of those who have died return to be with their families for a few hours. One of the preparations for the Day of the Dead is to make special kinds of bread and some of the foods that were the dead person's favourites when he or she was alive. The food is placed on an altar or taken to the cemetery and placed over the dead person's tomb. The souls are believed to return to the world to share a meal with their families.

Roadside altars like this one often have food on them as an offering to the souls of those who have died.

Mexican smoothie

Equipment

electric liquidizer
  or blender
a glass

Ingredients
Serves 1

1 ripe banana
200 ml milk
1 tablespoon
  honey
2 pinches
  cinnamon
  powder
3 drops vanilla
  essence

1   Put all the ingredients into
the jar of the liquidizer.

2   Cover the jar and liquidize
the ingredients until the
mixture is smooth. Pour into
a glass.

Make sure there is an
adult to help you
operate the liquidizer
or blender.

Salsa

Equipment

chopping board
knife
bowl
spoon

Ingredients
Serves 2 to 3

1 small onion or 6 to
   8 spring onions
2 large, very ripe
   tomatoes
juice of 1 lime
salt to taste
a few coriander leaves

1 Chop the onion or spring onions into small pieces.

Always ask an adult to help you when using a knife

2 Put the onion into the bowl and add the lime juice and a small amount of salt.

3 Wash the tomatoes and the coriander and chop them into small pieces. Add them into the bowl and mix with the spoon.

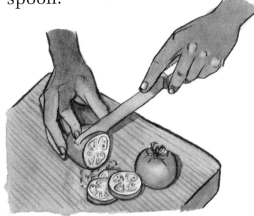

4 Allow the mixture to sit for five minutes and then taste it to see if it needs more salt. Serve with *quesadillas* (see page 21), *tacos,* grilled meat or fish, or as a 'dip'.

Guacamole

Equipment

chopping board
knife
bowl
spoon

Ingredients
Serves 2

1 large tomato
1 small onion
juice of 1 lime
salt to taste
1 large ripe
   avocado
a few coriander
   leaves

1 Wash the tomato and chop it into small pieces.

Always ask an adult
to help you when
using a knife.

2 Chop the onion finely.
Put it into the bowl with the
tomato. Add the lime juice
and some salt.

3 Wash and peel the
avocado. Cut it into small
pieces and add to the bowl.

4 Wash and chop the
coriander. Add to the bowl
and mix everything with the
spoon. Taste and add salt if
needed.

5 Serve *guacamole* as a 'dip'
at a party. You could buy
packets of *tortilla* chips for
people to dip into it and pop
into their mouths. Or make
tacos by filling *tortillas* with
guacamole. It is also delicious
served as a side dish with
grilled meat or boiled rice.

Mexican fruit snack

Equipment

knife
chopping board
bowl
spoon

Ingredients
Serves 2

1 medium-sized
    cucumber
1 ripe mango
1 orange
150 g papaya
100 g pineapple
juice of 1 lime
salt to taste

1　Wash and carefully peel all the fruits.

2　Cut the fruit into bite-sized pieces and put into the bowl. Mix with the spoon.

3　Sprinkle with salt and add the lime juice. Mix everything together and taste to see if it needs more salt.

Always ask an adult to help you when using a knife.

44

Glossary

Anise A small plant used to flavour food. The leaves and seeds, called aniseeds, taste like liquorice.

Aztecs The people who ruled most of the central and southern part of present-day Mexico before they were conquered by the Spanish. The Aztecs had an advanced civilization with huge pyramids, temples and palaces.

Baptism The ceremony used to admit a person, often a young baby, into the Christian Church. Part of the ceremony involves pouring water over the person's head.

Capital The city from where a country is governed.

Caterers People who provide and serve food at gatherings and parties.

Cereal Any grain, such as wheat, maize or rice, that is used for food.

Conquerors People who gain control, usually by force, over another group of people. The Spanish were conquerors of the native societies that lived in what is now Mexico.

Descendant A person who is the child or grandchild or great-grandchild, and so forth, of someone.

Diet The sort of food a person generally eats.

Dough A sticky paste made from flour and kneaded until it is elastic. Bread and wheat *tortillas* are made from dough.

Fertile When referring to soil, fertile means very rich and nourishing, thus helping plants to grow.

Grassland Land where grass is the main form of plant life.

Graze To feed on grass growing in fields.

Harvest The fruits, vegetables or grains that are picked at the end of a growing season.

Hibiscus A plant with small red flowers that grows in sandy soil. The flowers are used to flavour drinks.

Hoe A tool with a long handle and a thin flat blade at the end used for weeding and loosening the soil.

Hominy A whole, dried maize without the husk. It needs to be softened by boiling.

Iguana A large lizard with a row of spines from its neck to its tail, found in warm climates of North, Central and South America.

Indians The name the Europeans gave to the native peoples they found living in the Americas.

Knead To mix dough by folding over, pressing and squeezing it by hand.

Legend A story that is handed down through the generations and believed to have some truth, although it cannot be proved.

Mayas People who belong to the Indian peoples of the Yucatan area of Mexico. Before they were conquered by the Spanish, the Mayas had a highly developed civilization with beautiful art work and temples built on pyramids. Their knowledge of astronomy and mathematics was greater than any other culture at that time.

Medicinal Acting like medicines; able to cure illnesses.

Mennonite A member of the Mennonite Church, which was formed in Germany in the sixteenth century. Mennonites believe in plain, simple living. Today there are Mennonite farming communities in Europe and North America.

Mortar A very hard bowl in which substances are ground or pounded with a pestle.

Pestle A club-shaped tool used to pound or grind substances in a mortar.

Plough A tool used to break up and cut a groove in the soil so that it is ready for planting seeds.

Roman Catholics Members of the Roman Catholic Church, a Christian Church headed by the Pope.

Rural Of the countryside.

Savoury Having a salty or spicy taste; not sweet.

Tradition A custom or a way of doing something that has not changed for years.

Volcanic rock A fine-textured rock that forms when hot liquid lava from a volcano cooled down and hardened.

Books to read

The Cuisines of Mexico by Diana Kennedy (Harper and Row, 1986)

Food around the World by Ridgwell and Ridgeway (Oxford University Press, 1986)

Mexican Food and Drink by Manuel Alvarado (Wayland, 1988)

Mexico by Carmen Irizarry (Franklin Watts, 1986)

Mexico Is My Country by Bernice and Clifford Moon (Wayland, 1985)

Picture acknowledgements

The publishers would like to thank the following for allowing their photographs to be reproduced: Chapel Studios cover inset, 19, 21, 26, 39, 40, 42, 44; Greg Evans International *frontispiece* (Miwako Ikeda), 8 top, (Miwako Ikeda); Eye Ubiquitous 32 (G. Howe); Catarina Illsley 10 bottom, 12 bottom, 14 bottom, 17 bottom, 28, 30, 31 top right; Life File 12 top (Caroline Field), 29 (Juliet Highet); Tony Morrison: South American Pictures 6 bottom, 7 top, 9, 11, 13, 14 top, 15, 16 (Robert Francis), 18, 23 both, 25 (Kimbell Morrison) 31 top left and bottom, 34, 35 top, 38 both (Robert Francis); Tony Stone Worldwide cover, 4 (Robert Frerck), 6 top (Robert Frerck), 7 bottom (David Hiser), 8 bottom (David Hiser), 10 top, 24 top (Ken Fisher), 36 (David Hiser); Wayland Picture Library 17 top (Skjold), 24 bottom (John Wright), 27, 33, 35 bottom (John Wright), 37 (John Wright).

The map artwork on page 5 was supplied by Peter Bull. The recipe artwork on pages 19 to 22 and 39 to 44 was supplied by Judy Stevens.

Index